The power of the media

Why the media matter

The term 'the media' refers to a range of different methods of mass communication, sometimes called 'the mass media', because of their potential to communicate simultaneously with large groups of people.

There are three main types of media: print, broadcast and new media. Print media include newspapers, magazines, leaflets and posters. Broadcast media include TV, radio and film. **New media** refers to the text, images and audio material available on the internet.

The term 'media' can be defined as channels of communication society uses to speak about itself, making those who contribute to and control the media powerful members of society. One of the aims of this book is to look at the balance of power between media producers and media consumers. Because the media play such a crucial part in the way we perceive society, especially our political institutions such as parliament, a discussion of today's media will be central to any Citizenship course.

Local and global

You are surrounded by the media: at home, in the street, in the workplace, in shops, clubs and cinemas. The media vary in scope from local to global. A message on the 'lost and found' notice board in your local post office may reach a few dozen people, whereas a TV news bulletin broadcast on a global satellite channel, such as CNN, will reach millions.

Throughout the world, the media are playing an increasingly important role in everyone's life. They are helping to empower citizens, because they provide not only entertainment but also information and education. Thus, newspapers, magazines, radio, television and the internet all have a powerful impact on billions of people worldwide, helping to shape their perception of present, as well as past and future events.

TV news tries to be as up-to-the-minute as possible, often broadcasting reports as soon as they are researched

Shaping your world view

Rupert Murdoch's company News Corporation owns many of the smaller media companies from which we gather our information

As you can't possibly experience everything 'first hand', most of what you know about the world is the result of your exposure to various media. Billions of people worldwide, for instance, know what happened in New York on 11 September 2001. Because of satellite technology, they were able to watch the dramatic events unfold as they happened. Millions are able to describe the awful events in some detail, though only relatively few people actually *saw* in person what happened.

You are probably exposed to more mass media messages in one year than your great-grandparents were exposed to in their lifetime. However, to become an informed and active citizen, you need to appreciate the power of the media, how they can influence society, and shape your view of the world, locally and globally.

Discuss

1 In what ways would society today be different if modern media such as radio and television had *not* been invented?

2 How do the media empower people?

1

Broadcast media in the UK

UK television

There are five **analogue channels** for **terrestrial television** in the UK. BBC1 and BBC2 are funded by a licence fee; ITV, Channel 4 and Channel 5 are funded by advertising and sponsorship.

Satellite and cable services are mainly funded by subscription. The biggest satellite provider is British Sky Broadcasting (BSkyB).

UK TV Audience Share 2001

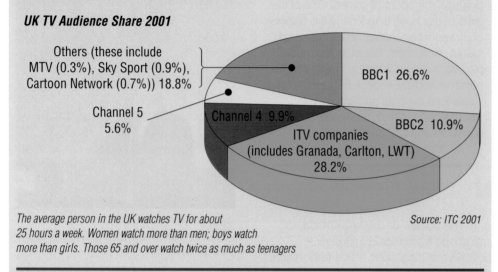

Others (these include MTV (0.3%), Sky Sport (0.9%), Cartoon Network (0.7%)) 18.8%

Channel 5 5.6%

Channel 4 9.9%

BBC1 26.6%

BBC2 10.9%

ITV companies (includes Granada, Carlton, LWT) 28.2%

Source: ITC 2001

The average person in the UK watches TV for about 25 hours a week. Women watch more than men; boys watch more than girls. Those 65 and over watch twice as much as teenagers

Cable and satellite services

Cable services are delivered to consumers by underground cable and paid for by subscription. 'Broadband cables' can carry up to 65 channels. Digital technology will allow a cable to carry up to 500 channels. Cable is also used for computer-based services, such as 'video-on-demand', home shopping, banking and high-speed internet access. It can also be used for local TV services.

Satellite services are delivered by satellite. The signal is transmitted from one point on the earth's surface, bounced off a satellite and received in another location.

When satellite broadcasts were launched in the UK in 1989, viewers had a choice of just four channels. In 1998, with the arrival of digital technology, this increased to 140. Satellite services are paid for by monthly subscription, and viewers need a set-top box to decode satellite signals. All satellite services in the UK are regulated by the ITC (see page 3).

Free-to-view and Pay-TV

Free-to-view (sometimes called 'free-to-air') TV channels are those which you don't have to pay an extra subscription to receive. Free-to-view channels include BBC, ITV, Channel 4, Channel 5, and some text, shopping and community channels. There is no such thing as a 'free' channel, of course. All BBC TV and radio channels are paid for indirectly by a licence fee, and commercial TV and radio are funded by the fees paid by companies advertising on these channels.

Pay-TV describes any TV channel you have to pay extra for. As well as normal subscription channels, Pay-TV includes other channels where you have to 'pay-per-view', that is you have to pay individually to watch particular films, one-off sports fixtures or other special events.

Teletext

There are a number of teletext services operated by both BBC and ITV companies, as well as Sky. They offer constantly updated information on such things as news, sport and travel. Over 15 million UK homes can receive these services. Licences for teletext services are awarded to commercial channels by ITC.

UK radio – national and local

As well as the eight national radio stations serving the UK (five BBC and three commercial), there are 39 local BBC stations and about 240 local commercial stations, broadcasting mainly sport and pop music, along with local news, weather and traffic updates.

BBC radio

BBC Network Radio transmits over 40 000 hours of programmes per year at present, and plans to introduce five additional radio services by 2002. These are available via satellite, cable and the internet.

Independent radio

There are currently three independent national radio services that broadcast 24 hours a day: Classic FM, Virgin 1215 and Talk Sport.

Independent local radio stations broadcast a wide range of news, sport and music programmes. They include stations which cater for ethnic minority audiences, as well as services aimed at specific local 'populations', such as students and hospital patients.

Discuss

1 Do we need so many radio and television channels?

2 What would happen if we had fewer channels?

Media organizations

The government department responsible for all UK broadcast media is the Department of Culture, Media and Sport. This department is responsible for three key media organizations.

The British Broadcasting Corporation (BBC)

The BBC broadcasts TV, radio, and on-line services, and is the UK's main public service broadcaster. BBC services are funded almost exclusively by a licence fee – approximately £100 per year, per household. It broadcasts 17 000 hours of television per year on its analogue channels, BBC1 and BBC2. It also provides a range of free-to-air digital services (BBC News 24, BBC Choice, BBC4, two children's channels and BBC Parliament).

The BBC was first formed as a company in 1922. In 1927 it was granted its first Royal Charter, which sets out the company's "purposes, powers and duties".

Under the charter, the BBC is independent of political control – even though most of its funds come from the government (the licence fee). One of the BBC's main duties is as a public service broadcaster, producing programmes funded by the taxpayer, aimed at a wide audience.

BBC World Service

This global radio service broadcasts mainly news and current affairs programmes in over 40 languages to an estimated weekly audience of 153 million listeners.

BBC Worldwide

This BBC company is Europe's largest exporter of TV programmes, the world's biggest TV operator outside the USA, and the UK's third largest publisher of consumer magazines. It operates 12 commercial channels in the UK and overseas, which together reach over 350 million households worldwide. In 2001, BBC Worldwide reinvested £96 million in programming and other services.

The Independent Television Commission (ITC)

The ITC does not make or transmit programmes, but is a **public watchdog**. Its job is to ensure that a wide range of commercial TV is available throughout the UK, and that it is of high quality and will appeal to a variety of tastes. Programme content, advertising and technical standards are all governed by an ITC code. The ITC must also ensure that the rules applying to media ownership are complied with (see pages 6 and 7). The ITC regulates all commercial TV, including cable and satellite.

Independent Television Commission

PUTTING VIEWERS FIRST

Independent Television (ITV)

ITV (or Channel 3) is made up of 15 regionally-based commercial TV companies, all licensed and controlled by the ITC. These licences are awarded for a 10-year period. Companies who bid for these licences must offer programmes that appeal to a wide range of tastes and interests. For example, about one third of programmes must be news, documentaries, current affairs and education.

Channel 4 and Channel 5

Channel 4 is a national commercial service, also controlled by ITC. Its remit is to cater for audiences not generally catered for by ITV. Channel 5, the UK's newest commercial TV channel, which began broadcasting in 1997, reaches 70% of the population.

The Radio Authority

The Radio Authority regulates commercial radio, including cable and satellite radio. It controls and allocates the frequencies on which stations can broadcast, grants licences and monitors programme content.

Ofcom

By the end of 2003 there are plans for one single organization - Ofcom - to act as a media 'watchdog'. Ofcom will be made up from the Independent Television Commission, the Broadcasting Standards Commission, The Radio Authority, Oftel and the Radiocommunications Agency.

The 15 regionally based commercial TV companies

Discuss

1 Why do we need 'watchdogs' such as the ITC?

2 Do you think public service broadcasting is a good thing?

3 "The BBC is important because it uses taxpayers' money to provide programmes for a wide range of audiences. If we only had commercial TV, the range of programmes would be limited." Do you agree with this view?

Print media in the UK

The press

On an average weekday over half the adult population of the UK will read a national morning paper. Newspaper circulation is declining, but total daily circulation still stands at around 13 million on weekdays, and 14 million on Sunday. Newspapers are the largest UK advertising medium, making a major contribution to the national economy.

Each of these national newspapers takes a different 'angle' when representing a story to its readers

National newspapers

Hundreds of different newspapers are published in the UK every week. There are two main types of national newspaper: **tabloid** and **broadsheet**. Broadsheets – so-called because of their large page size – include *The Daily Telegraph*, *The Times* and *The Guardian*. Tabloids have smaller pages – half the size of broadsheets. The two most popular UK daily papers, *The Sun* and *The Daily Mirror*, are both tabloids.

A number of national papers appear only on a Sunday. There are four Sunday broadsheets and five Sunday tabloids. The tabloid *News of the World* sells about four million copies, making it the UK's top-selling title, as well as the top-selling Sunday paper.

The tabloids sell up to four times as many copies as the broadsheets. The other main differences between tabloids and broadsheets are:

- design and layout – tabloids contain more pictures, bigger headlines and shorter stories

- content – tabloids may concentrate more on stories about crime, sex and 'celebrity scandal'. Broadsheets tend to give background analysis of stories, which are more likely to be about major political and economic affairs, than 'human interest' stories.

UK newspapers: average net circulation for April 2002	
The Sun	3 351 648
The Daily Mail	2 446 197
Daily Mirror	2 108 530
The Daily Telegraph	1 006 380
Daily Express	907 772
The Times	717 281
The Guardian	404 630
The Independent	226 584

Audit Bureau of Circulation 2002

David and Victoria Beckham are tabloid favourites and receive lots of press coverage

Regional news outlets

As well as the national newspapers produced in London, there are many regional titles produced throughout the UK. Most large towns and cities have their own regional or local papers. These mainly deal with stories that have local or regional appeal, but occasionally will cover national and international events, looked at from a local perspective. Around 90 per cent of local and **regional titles** are now also available online.

Regional newspapers are an important source of news for many people. More than 40 per cent of adults who read a local paper never read a national daily. Nearly 85 per cent of adults in the UK read a regional paper, making them the most widely read medium in the country, outstripping both magazines and national newspapers. They generate a huge amount of advertising revenue.

Very few of the regional dailies are morning papers; most go on sale in the evening. Glasgow's *Daily Record* is the UK's top selling regional daily with a circulation of 600 000 copies. The *London Evening Standard* sells around 500 000.

There are over 600 free papers published every week in the UK, the best known of which is probably *Metro*. Launched in 1999, it distributes over 800 000 copies every weekday to commuters in London and seven other major cities. Another London-based free paper, *Newsquest*, has a circulation of over one million.

Ethnic minority press

There are a growing number of newspapers and magazines aimed specifically at ethnic minorities. Most are published weekly or less frequently, but a few like the *Daily Jang*, are dailies. The *Asian Times* is an English-language paper, but other titles appear in Bengali, Gujarati, Hindi and Punjabi. There are also publications aimed at Chinese and Afro-Caribbean communities.

Magazines

The easiest way to get a clear idea of the scope and scale of the UK print media is to visit a large newsagent. Apart from a range of daily and Sunday newspapers, you will see displayed a vast array of magazines. There are over 9000 different magazines published in the UK, about 5000 of which are business and professional publications. These are not aimed at the general reader. Many are 'in-house' publications produced by public services or companies, and aimed at employees and customers, so most don't appear on the newsagent's shelves alongside more general, consumer magazines such as *Just Seventeen* and *The Radio Times*.

Magazines rely very heavily on advertising. They are relatively cheap to produce, compared with newspapers. Because they are produced weekly or monthly, they can never be as topical as newspapers, but focus instead on feature articles, reviews and interviews. Women's magazines have high circulation figures – *Woman* and *Woman's Own* sell over half a million copies per issue – and newer titles aimed at men, such as *FHM* and *Loaded*, also sell well.

Discuss

1 How would you explain the enduring appeal of regional newspapers?

2 "Tabloids ceased being newspapers a long time ago. They don't give their readers news; they give them gossip, tittle-tattle and speculation." Would you describe the tabloids as newspapers?

Just some of the many magazines published in the UK

Who owns the media?

Media groups

Today many media outlets belong to larger media companies. This means that many newspapers, magazines or television companies are not run separately and independently. Instead, they are controlled by the larger media company. In the UK, these large media companies include Trinity Mirror, Associated Newspapers, Pearson and News Corporation. Large media companies can be national or international businesses. International businesses are known as 'multinationals' because they have businesses in more than one country.

There is concern about the power these large media companies have and so they are controlled by competition laws and ownership regulations. Some people worry that if one single company owns too many media outlets, it could be in a position to influence public opinion. For example, if all newspapers in one country were owned by one group, they could print biased stories and there would be no other newspaper available to show another point of view.

Who owns what? UK Daily and Sunday Newspapers	
News Corporation:	*The Times, The Sunday Times, The Sun* and *News of the World.* Plus large part of BSkyB.
Trinity Mirror:	*The Daily Mirror, The Sunday Mirror* and *The Sunday People*
Associated Newspapers:	*The Daily Mail, Mail on Sunday* and *London Evening Standard.* Plus 20% share of Independent Television News (ITN).
Guardian Media Group:	*The Guardian* and *The Observer*
Hollinger New Telegraph New Media:	*The Daily Telegraph*
Independent News and Media:	*The Independent*

Discuss

1 Why have some people expressed concerns about large multinational companies taking over media organizations? In your opinion, are these fears justified?

2 Why does a media group like Disney want to own shops, hotels, cruise ships and theme parks?

The Disney Empire: an example of global cross-media ownership

- Owns or part-owns more than ten international broadcasting channels including The Disney Channel

- Broadcasts in the UK and seven other countries, across Europe and South America

- Owns ABC TV and radio networks – ten television stations and 29 radio stations in the USA

- Owns five TV production and distribution companies

- Owns eight online companies, including Disney Interactive, which develops and markets computer software, video/DVD, games and CDs

- Owns five magazine publishing companies and three book publishing companies

- Owns four daily newspapers

- Owns six record/music companies

- Owns seven theme parks and resorts including Disneyland, Anaheim

Disney, MGM Studios, Disneyland Paris, Walt Disney World, Disney's Animal Kingdom (Orlando, Florida), Walt Disney's World Sports Complex, The California Adventure Park

- Owns 27 hotels with over 36 000 rooms

- Owns Disney Cruise Line (two cruise ships)

- Owns Disney Stores, with over 720 shops worldwide

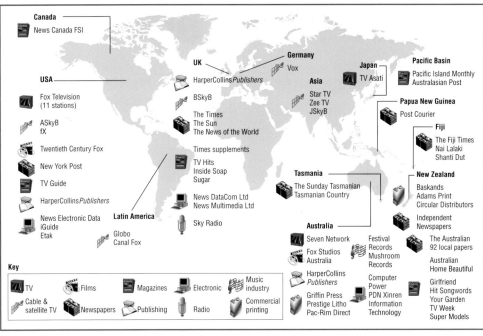

Companies that are owned, or partly owned, by News Corporation, a multinational media company

Independent media institutions

Not all media outlets are owned by large media groups. There are independent publishing companies which publish, for example, magazines and periodicals. Also, at the other end of the spectrum from multinationals are small groups producing 'fanzines' or community-based media products. They are often more local in their outlook and use local technology to produce their publications.

With the increasing availability of the internet, small groups can use it as a way of reaching their audiences. Before the internet, a particular interest group would have had to print a newsletter or magazine. Now, the internet potentially provides a cheaper way of distributing the same type of information to a much larger audience.

The Gareth Gates website is an internet-based fanzine, instead of the traditional print-based fanzine

The Jericho Echo is an Oxford based community media product which has a locally-based readership

Discuss

In future, foreign media companies may take over UK commercial television and radio channels. Do you think this would be a good or bad thing?

UK media ownership regulations

Anyone can launch a newspaper in the UK and you don't need a licence to work as a journalist, but **cross-media ownership** is strictly regulated. This means a company can't have a significant stake in several different media organizations, for example, newspapers and TV stations.

Up until 2002, the Broadcasting Act of 1996 regulated all cross-media ownership in the UK. Under this law, any company that controlled more than 20 per cent of national newspaper circulation could not own more than a 20 per cent stake in any ITV company or Channel 5. No one commercial TV company could have more than 15 per cent of the total TV audience. Cross-media ownership was controlled in this way to ensure power was not concentrated in too few hands in an anti-competitive way, and to promote a range of views, especially in news programmes.

In 2002, the government proposed changes to the 1996 Act. The draft Electronic Communications Bill will relax the rules governing cross-media ownership and allow foreign media companies to buy UK commercial television and radio channels. Global giants such as AOL Time Warner and Disney could, in future, take over companies such as Granada and Carlton TV.

The Bill also proposes the creation of a unified regulatory body, Ofcom – the Office of Communications – which will take over the work of the Broadcast Standards Commission, the ITC and the Radio Authority (see page 3).

Regulating the BBC

The BBC's charter sets out how the company is to be run. The director-general is in overall, day-to-day control of the company – in much the same way that a managing director runs any large business. The work of the director-general and the rest of the senior managers at the BBC is overseen by 12 part-time governors. BBC managers and governors meet every month.

Who decides the news agenda?

Gatekeepers

Perhaps the single most important thing we must remember about the media is that they are highly selective. Of all the events worldwide which might be thought of as 'newsworthy', only a fraction is reported in newspapers or TV news bulletins. As there isn't time or space to include every story, editors and others who shape the news act as **gatekeepers**. It is they who decide which stories to include. It is they who control the flow of news and the way it is presented.

Because all media are selective, a particular TV programme, magazine or newspaper article or website doesn't present us with 'the truth'. Rather it provides a version of the truth, shaped by a host of factors. For example, two investigative journalists both writing about the crash which killed Diana, Princess of Wales, could produce two very different articles, depending on who they interviewed, what access they had to police files and other sensitive materials, the amount of time they spent researching the story, and the newspaper audience they were writing for (**tabloid** or **broadsheet**). Even their personal feelings about the monarchy might influence the tone of their article.

All media messages are 'constructed' by journalists, photographers, film crews, editors and others. We see the finished advert or news bulletin, so we rarely see what was rejected by those who constructed the message. In this way news editors 'shape' the news. The stories you read in your paper or see on your TV are the stories a small number of **gatekeepers** have selected for you.

Editorials

In most newspapers you will find an editorial – sometimes referred to as a leading article or 'leader'. This is written by the paper's editor and contains comments on one or more of the major stories of the day. If the editorial is a comment on a political story, the opinions expressed will usually, but not always, reflect the political leaning of the paper. Because of this, the comments in an editorial are likely to be in keeping with the views of the paper's owner and not simply the editor's personal opinions.

The role of editors

Television news editors decide which will be the 'lead story', the order in which the stories will be presented (the running order) and how much airtime each story will have. These selections inevitably reflect the values and priorities of the editors and their colleagues. One editor may choose to lead with a story about the royal family, whilst another may give more time and space to a political story. Their choice may be influenced in part by their audience. The early evening news is watched by more children than late-night bulletins, and the audience for midday, midweek bulletins will include more retired people. These are all factors which will influence the composition of news programmes. Editorial choices may also be influenced by the availability of pictures to accompany the story (see page 12).

In the same way, newspaper editors determine which stories will go on the front page, with supporting pictures and graphics, and which will be relegated to the inside pages. These choices are influenced by the papers' readership profiles, that is the average age, income, jobs, interests and political views of its readers. A tabloid editor may use just a single, dramatic photograph with a one-word headline on the front page as a 'hook' for a story on the inside pages.

Commercial interests

The majority of media messages are prompted by commercial interests. Except for the BBC, which is funded by public money, all media organizations are businesses driven by the need to make profits. Without selling advertising space, these businesses couldn't run. This brings in revenue for the publishers, but also means the price of the magazine is kept affordable for the buyer.

Today's teenagers, who spend over £8 billion a year on magazines, have much more disposable income compared to previous generations, so businesses are keen to target this readership via magazine adverts. Over half of magazine profits and one third of newspaper profits are the result of advertising revenue. Newspapers will lay out their pages with adverts first, before filling the 'gaps' with news. Programmes on commercial television are made primarily to entertain, but have the secondary function of creating an audience for the companies that advertise during these programmes.

The Radio Times charges advertisers nearly £20 000 for a full page advert

The influence of the US tobacco industry on US media

Because editors are so important, it is understandable that powerful commercial and political groups may try to influence their decisions. The tobacco industry in the USA is a case in point. It spends over $5 billion a year on advertising, and since cigarette adverts on radio and TV were banned in the USA in 1970, most of this money is now spent on adverts in the print media.

In 1994, a survey of American magazines that carry tobacco adverts revealed that over 90% of these publications were worried that tobacco companies would withdraw their adverts from magazines that included anti-smoking messages. The majority of magazines surveyed were also concerned that the tobacco producers' parent companies might also withdraw their non-tobacco adverts. Philip Morris, one of the world's biggest tobacco companies, also owns Kraft and General Foods.

Adapted from adbusters.org

Politics and the press

In the same way that you might support a particular football team, some newspapers have historically supported the policies of a particular political party. *The Daily Telegraph*, for example, was more likely to support Conservative policies than *The Guardian*, which leaned towards Labour. Nowadays, the political affiliation of a particular newspaper is less predictable. A paper may be pro-Labour on matters relating to Europe, but anti-Labour in its stand on law and order.

Newspaper support for New Labour and the Conservative Party during the 1997 General Election

New Labour: *The Guardian, The Independent, The Financial Times, The Daily Mirror, The Sun* and *The Daily Star*

Conservative: *The Daily Telegraph, The Daily Express* and *The Daily Mail*

During a general election newspapers may urge their readers to vote for a particular party

It would be too simplistic to say that a newspaper's readers vote according to that paper's politics. Are the political opinions of *Telegraph* readers shaped by what they read in the paper? Or do they read that particular newspaper because it reflects the political views they already hold?

It is very important that people have access to more than one newspaper. It is important also that the press reflects a wide range of political opinions. If some papers support government policies on crime and education, it is vital in a democracy that readers have access to other papers that question these policies.

Discuss

"There's nothing wrong with adverts – they keep the price of the magazines down and they mean TV companies can produce a variety of shows." How far do you agree with this view?

How much does Europe trust its newspapers?

According to an EU-wide poll conducted in November 2000, only 20 per cent of UK citizens trust what they read in UK newspapers. This was the lowest figure of all the 15 EU countries surveyed. In Germany and Italy, the figure was 40 per cent and in France, it was 60 per cent.

There are important differences between UK newspapers and those published in other EU countries, where it is unusual for a paper to ally itself with a particular political party, as some UK papers have done. There is less competition for readers between papers in both France and Germany. They are less interested in headline-grabbing, sensational stories, and more concerned with analysis and explanation.

In France, Italy and Spain there aren't daily tabloids in the same style as *The Sun* or *The Mirror*, and the few tabloids published in the EU tend not to blur the boundaries between news and entertainment, as UK tabloids do. In short, there is a more serious approach to news in both the tabloids and broadsheets.

Discuss

1 Do you think newspapers tell the truth?

2 If newspapers aren't to be trusted, are there any other sources of information you can rely on?

3 How much influence do you think newspapers have on people's political views – a little or a lot? Say why.

Politicians, public relations and the media

Spin and spin-doctors

Some politicians employ press officers and political advisers – often referred to as **spin-doctors**. Their job is to make sure the message politicians want to get across is seen in the best possible light by the public, in other words, the voters. Their principal role is news management – they manipulate the news agenda.

For example, say there is a report about to be published giving figures of the clear-up rates for crime. The report states that while 66 per cent of criminal offences remain unsolved, 33 per cent are cleared up – an increase from the previous year when only 23 per cent of crimes were cleared up. The story could be given a positive spin by emphasizing the rise in clear-up rates, in the hope that the media would focus on that aspect of the report with headlines such as "Big increase in crimes that are cleared up", rather than negative headlines such as "Two thirds of crimes remain unsolved".

Public relations firms

In the same way that politicians want to deliver news stories at good moments, so too do private businesses. In the City of London's Stock Exchange, an important centre of international finance, stocks and shares are bought and sold according to how well particular companies are performing.

One way a company can increase the value of its shares is by demonstrating that it is a company worth investing in. Companies therefore employ **public relations firms (PR)** to promote the successes of the company in the hope that people will invest in it. If a company doesn't employ an external PR firm, it may have its own internal PR department.

One of the main aims of a PR company is to market its clients' businesses. In other words, they are like advertising agencies for business, and they use the media to gain publicity by providing press releases to news agencies, newspapers, TV and radio.

Business and the media

The Stock Exchange has its own 'regulatory news service' and companies are supposed to release any news which might affect their value on the Stock Exchange through it. This is so that access to information about a company's performance is available simultaneously to all stockbrokers, both in London and internationally. Also, by having an official news service, it is hoped that all stories are accurate and honest.

In 2001, the Financial Services Authority introduced stricter guidelines to PR companies as it was concerned about the way some PR companies were releasing sensitive information to the national press before going through the Stock Exchange's news service. This was happening through a process called the 'Friday night drop'. The Stock Exchange's news service closes at 6.30pm on Fridays, and PR companies were 'leaking' stories to the national press after this time so that the stories would appear in the national Sunday papers. Some PR companies argued that this was the most reliable way of getting information to private investors, but the FSA were worried that misleading stories about particular businesses were being leaked, thus breaching fair competition and trade regulations.

Spin-doctors

Senior politicians of all parties have always used civil servants as advisers. Recently, however, there has been some concern about how powerful a certain type of civil servant – spin-doctors – have become. Unlike MPs, they are unelected and not accountable to the public via the ballot box, and unlike their political masters, they keep out of the public eye.

Political adviser Jo Moore

Jo Moore, a political adviser in the Department of Trade and Industry, hit the headlines in 2001 when it was revealed she had sent an e-mail to her colleagues within minutes of the terrorist attack on the World Trade Center on 11 September, saying "today would be a very good day to bury bad news". Many thought this was spin gone too far.

Discuss

1 Do you think it is right that politicians use spin-doctors?

2 "People who work in the PR business are paid to tell lies." Say whether you agree or disagree, and explain why.

Politics on TV

The five main terrestrial TV channels (BBC1, BBC2, ITV, Channel 4 and Channel 5) broadcast 24 hours a day, seven days a week – 840 hours in total, but less than one per cent of this output is devoted to political programmes.

When Parliament is in session, there are daily live broadcasts from Westminster, including Prime Minister's Question Time, on BBC2. These may be extended to cover emergency debates such as the one following the 11 September terrorist attack on New York. There is regular continuous coverage on cable, satellite and digital TV, but this attracts a very small audience. Two parliamentary websites also allow you to view debates as they happen.

HECTOR BREEZE

"I'm not only being tagged but I've got to watch 100 hours of old party conference tapes."

There are strict rules governing how debates in parliament are televised, so viewers get a balance. For example, the programme director is not allowed to show an MP who may have fallen asleep during a lengthy speech – even though this does happen.

The amount of politics you are able to see via broadcast media is actually a small proportion of the business of parliament, most of which goes on in private meetings. This means what we can see and hear directly on TV and radio is very much an edited product. A news bulletin may reduce a lengthy parliamentary debate to a 20-second 'sound bite'.

Party's over for politics on TV

The BBC is considering dramatically scaling down its live coverage of party conferences because not enough people are tuning in.

BBC2 has, for years, carried many hours of broadcasts. But they could be replaced by daily highlights, with only the party leaders' speeches broadcast live.

Although TV soaps such as *EastEnders* can have as many as 12 million viewers, party conferences struggle to get one million – with the core audience of under-45s the least likely to tune in.

The changes reflect growing political apathy. Last year, only 59% of those eligible voted in the general election – the lowest since 1918.

Adapted from The Daily Express, 1 March 2002

Party political broadcasts

Party Political Broadcasts (PPBs) are used by political parties, usually just before general or local elections, to explain their policies to voters or to attack the policies of opposing parties. They are broadcast on both BBC and commercial television, and on various radio stations.

To qualify for a PPB, a party must contest at least 15 per cent of the seats in the election. There are strict guidelines on the content of PPBs:

- no PPB can be used to ask viewers to donate money to the party

- if they employ actors, this must be made clear to the audience

- broadcasts must also comply with the laws on libel, privacy, racial discrimination, etc.

Plans for American-style PPBs

One suggestion to tackle voter apathy has been to replace party political broadcasts with American-style election adverts. In the US, political candidates run 30-second advertising slots, and supporters of the idea think that this kind of campaign would appeal more to voters. Critics point out that shorter broadcasts don't necessarily mean more interest – in the US, voter turnout is lower than in the UK. Also, the short format of these adverts would mean policies wouldn't be explained clearly and political parties might end up concentrating on spin and presentation over substance. There is the additional worry that short broadcasts tend to focus on **negative campaigning** about the opposition party, rather than focusing on issues which are of concern to the public.

Discuss

1 What should the media be doing (if anything) to try to combat voter apathy?

2 Should party political broadcasts become shorter and more like American-style election broadcasts?

What makes a story newsworthy?

Why one particular story, rather than a dozen others that break on the same day, should be the front-page story in a newspaper or the lead story in a TV bulletin depends on a number of factors. It may be what journalists call a **human interest story** – "Brave 7-year-old rescues 4-year-old sister from a house fire". It may relate to a matter of national importance – the threat of war in the Middle East. Or it may concern a celebrity – a pop star, sports personality or politician involved in some kind of scandal.

Readers usually judge front-page stories to be more important than those buried inside the paper. TV and radio news bulletins run the most important stories first, and give them more airtime, and leave less significant items for later. Where a story is placed within a news bulletin or paper influences what a reader or viewer thinks about its importance.

Discuss

1 What do you think makes a story newsworthy?

2 "Stories about world events should always be given more coverage than stories about celebrities and sports." Discuss this view.

Broadsheet versus tabloid treatment

The same story will often be treated very differently by tabloid and broadsheet newspapers. A newspaper's approach to a story, in the main, reflects the importance editors believe their readers will attach to the story. For example, England's defeat by Brazil in the 2002 World Cup was covered by all UK newspapers. The Times (a broadsheet) put the story on its front page, but its main story was about the threat to British tourists to Spain from ETA, the Basque separatist group.

The front page of The Sun (a tabloid), by comparison, was filled with a single photograph of David Beckham consoling a tearful England goalkeeper, David Seaman, with the headline: "It's a crying shame". Inside, The Sun devoted four full pages to the story.

TV news and pictures

In June 2002, a huge forest fire raged across a large area of Colorado and spread to the neighbouring state of Arizona. TV news reports of the fire showed dramatic pictures of flames engulfing forests, and fire crews fighting the blaze. Because this region is only sparsely populated, relatively few, if any, lives were at risk.

At the same time, one million Indian and Pakistani soldiers were massed in the border of the Kashmir, and their generals and politicians were talking of the prospect of a nuclear war that could wipe out millions of people on the Indian subcontinent.

Because of the dramatic pictures, the forest fire was given a prominent place in most TV news bulletins at the time. The pictures from Kashmir, by comparison, were much less dramatic – sober-faced politicians going in and out of meetings – so the story was given less prominence.

It is often instructive to compare radio and TV news bulletins for the same day, to see how the running order of news items is sometimes dictated by the pictures that accompany items. England's exit from the 2002 World Cup, for example, was the first item on BBC and ITV news, with dramatic pictures of the goals in slow motion and from three or four different camera angles accompanying the commentator's frantic voice-over. The same event was reported in less detail on BBC Radio 4 news and was the fourth item in the bulletin.

Which of these two images would help make a good story?

Fast and slow news

Charles: Look out for your own kids!

Prince in drug sensation

Harry's Drug Shame

Cocaine shame of royal circle

"Harry's drug shame" is an example of a **fast news** story. It broke very quickly and was picked up immediately by all the other papers. There was further coverage in many papers the next day, but within a couple of days it had disappeared altogether from all UK newspapers.

When reporters descend en masse on a story like this it is often referred to as a **media feeding frenzy** – an allusion perhaps to the way sharks close in on and devour their prey. Deborah Orr's comment column, in *The Independent* on the day after the story broke carried the headline "Another media feeding frenzy". She argued that the media should have used the incident to start a sensible debate about young people and drugs, but that they failed miserably: "This story is about the media, sensation, intrusiveness, irresponsibility, cruelty. It's about splash, the feature back-up, the columnists, first-person accounts…The British press has camped out…on a teenager's psyche…"

By comparison, an example of **slow news** would be the way the UK media have reported the prospect of Britain giving up the pound and adopting the euro. There has been a long-running, but low-key, discussion in the media of the Chancellor of the Exchequer's five economic tests. Only when the government decides to hold a referendum on whether or not to join the euro, will the issue become fast news and dominate all news media.

Spin-doctors have been accused of news management, keeping some stories back in order to create a slow news day, so that one item – the one they would like in the media spotlight – becomes more prominent (see page 10, and *Democracy in Action*, page 23).

A global media event

The funeral of Diana, Princess of Wales, is thought to have been seen by 2.5 billion people worldwide – the largest audience in TV history. It was the biggest outside-broadcast the BBC had ever undertaken, involving 100 cameras and 300 technicians. Pictures from inside and outside Westminster Abbey were fed to 50 other networks and broadcast to 187 countries. Giant TV screens were erected in Hyde Park for the crowds who could not get near the funeral route.

Peter Barnard, ex-editor of *The Times* newspaper, explains why he thinks Diana's death was "the news story of the century".

"In the first week of September 1997, more than a hundred magazines in Britain and America alone, and countless more around the world, had on their covers a photograph of Diana, Princess of Wales. But the subject this time was not her sex appeal or her battles with slimming-related food disorders. The reason, in that momentous week, was that she was dead…

Wars, assassination, moon landings and sundry disasters can fairly be said to have been more significant and important in this century than the death of a princess. But significance and importance are not the only measures of a story. That is why I would nominate the death of Diana as the most stunning single news story of the century. If that seems like an overstatement, a surrender to **hype**, I can only argue that Diana was, surely, the most famous woman in the world and that her death at the age of 36 was an extraordinary shock for hundreds of millions of people. Issues arose at the time to do with whether we really ought to be so focused on a single

individual with no real power over our lives, a woman of privilege and wealth whose persona often seemed to be the creation of the media. But that is to tackle the reasons why Diana was famous. The fact that she was so famous is what made her death a stupendous event."

'We interrupt this programme', *by Peter Barnard*

Discuss

1 What kinds of events often result in a media 'feeding frenzy' and why?

2 Overall, is this level of media attention a good or bad thing?

News reports: true, fair and accurate?

Bias in the news

All journalists, in whatever medium they are working, have to make countless decisions every day: decisions concerning what to include and what to leave out of a story or article, what pictures to use, what captions to attach to them, what headlines to use. In this sense, all reporting is **biased reporting**. The finished report is the product of a number of personal choices, and not an objective account. Bias is an inevitable consequence of reporting any event. This book, like any other, will have its biases. The author and editor had to make numerous decisions about what to include, what emphases to give various facts, which illustrations and diagrams to use.

Not all bias is deliberate. It can creep into a news bulletin for example, principally through selection. An editor can express a bias by choosing to use, or not to use, a specific news item. With any particular story, some details can be ignored, and others included, to give a different slant to the events reported.

Bias through omission is more difficult to detect. Only by comparing news reports from a wide variety of outlets can this form of bias be observed. On the right are two versions of the same story – one from a tabloid, the other from a broadsheet. Compare the facts contained in each and the overall impression each report creates of the crash. How does the eyewitness comment influence your perception of the crash?

11 hurt in rail crash

ELEVEN people were injured yesterday when a train hit a lorry on an unmanned level crossing.

The train was thrown into the air but landed back on the track while the lorry ended up in a ditch.

Nine passengers and the two crew were taken to hospital after the crash near Saxmundham in Suffolk. Witness, John Patrick, 29, said, "There was a huge bang. It is lucky no one was killed."

Adapted from The Daily Mirror, *16 April 2002*

11 injured as train derailed

ELEVEN people were slightly injured when a train was derailed after crashing into an articulated lorry on a barrier-less level crossing at Blaxhall, Suffolk, yesterday.

Only the front axle of the single-carriage diesel train from Lowestoft to Ipswich came off the rails.

Adapted from The Daily Telegraph, *16 April 2002*

Accurate reporting

There are a number of reasons why a news report might be incomplete or inaccurate. The reporter may have got their facts wrong. If they'd been sent to report on an earthquake, they might have had problems getting near the site. Those in charge of the rescue might have been too preoccupied to speak to reporters. If people had been killed or badly injured, the reporter might have chosen to omit details of the worst injuries, knowing relatives and friends of the injured might read the report. In these situations, it is often weeks or months before all the facts concerning the disaster are known. Until all the facts are available, any report will be incomplete.

Can deliberate bias be acceptable?

There are occasions when news reports have been deliberately distorted. There is a well-known saying: "The first casualty of war is the truth". During World War I, *The Times* newspaper deliberately played down the horrific casualty figures from battlefields such as the Somme. More recently, reporting of the Falklands conflict and the Gulf War was restricted by the government.

Most people would accept that some wartime restrictions on reporting are necessary. Details of casualties, or of the movements of troops and planes,

for instance, could be useful to an enemy. But in a peacetime democracy, the media must be free to report without political interference. If government economic policies aren't working, and unemployment is rising, the media must be free to report this. If drug-related crime is increasing and experts are criticizing the government and the police, this should be reported fully and fairly.

This doesn't mean to say that journalists can write or say anything they like. There are legal limits on all

reporters. Anti-terrorism laws, libel laws and laws relating to how court cases are reported – the law of 'contempt' – may all limit what a reporter can say or write.

Discuss

1 Can a newspaper report ever be described as a 'true' account of an event?

2 Would reading two or more newspapers help readers to get a more accurate picture of events?

Reporting the war

Below are extracts from the BBC's guidelines to its reporters on reporting the war in Afghanistan, following the terrorist attacks of 11 September 2001:

● matters involving risk to, and loss of, life need handling with the utmost regard to the mood and feeling of our audiences. We must be sensitive to their feelings and fears

● many will have relatives or friends involved in the conflict. We will need to handle painful stories sensitively and with care

● we must avoid giving any impression that this is a war against Islam. The position taken by Osama Bin Laden and other Muslim extremists is not shared by the majority of Muslims, who would argue that it is contrary to Islamic teaching

● reports should normally make it absolutely clear where their information has come from, and attribute it accordingly

● enabling the national debate remains a vital task: the concept of impartiality still applies. All views should be reflected in due proportion to mirror the depth and spread of opinion

● we must reflect any significant opposition in the UK (and elsewhere) to the military conflict and allow their arguments to be heard and tested

● those who speak and perhaps demonstrate against war are to be reported as part of the national and international reality.

The Afghan War was reported worldwide. Here, a Mujahedin commander informs international journalists that Nangarhar is clear of al-Qaeda fighters

The influence of pictures

The pictures chosen to accompany a story can influence the way that story is perceived. This is particularly important in TV news, which can employ full-colour moving images. The captions attached to newspaper photographs can also influence readers' perceptions. Also, it is possible to manipulate photographs.

Distorting the truth

On October 1996, the National Union of Journalists (NUJ) launched a campaign to ensure that every time a **digitally-manipulated photograph** is used in a newspaper or magazine, one of the following symbols must appear within the picture to indicate if it has been digitally-manipulated.

NUJ symbol indicating an unmanipulated image   *NUJ symbol indicating a manipulated image*

When the *London Evening Standard* ran a photo of the Labour MP John Prescott with a beer bottle removed to justify the caption "champagne socialist", the NUJ called this "the first clearly party-political abuse of photo-manipulation in the UK".

The quality of digitally-manipulated images is so high that the NUJ symbol is needed to identify when an image has been altered

Freedom and censorship

A free press: the public's watchdog

If a democracy is to function effectively, all its citizens must have free access to information, and in an open society newspapers must be free to express a wide range of ideas and opinions. They provide the means for a variety of voices to be heard. At a national and local level, a free press is the public's watchdog.

One basic human right, set out in the Universal Declaration of Human Rights, is the right to free speech. Article 19 says: "Everyone has the right to the freedom of opinion and expression; this right includes freedom to hold opinions without interference and to seek, receive and impart information and ideas through any media and regardless of frontiers." This means you have a right to read a free press - not one controlled or **censored** by the government.

In a democracy, the government is the servant of the people – not vice versa. If the people don't agree with what the government is doing, the government can be voted out of power. But a totalitarian or undemocratic state will not tolerate a free press, so the people are starved of information.

Free for all?

How much official information should the average citizen have access to? When you start work, you will pay income tax and national insurance. This money is used by the government, on your behalf, to pay for services such as schools, police, the armed forces and hospitals. Because it is your money, you have a right to know how it is spent.

There is a great deal of information posted on official government websites. By simply typing in your postcode, you can access a range of statistical information about your local area, such as its demographic make-up, birth and death rates, the number of people claiming housing benefit or the number of registered disabled people.

Most people would agree it is reasonable for the government to record data on births and death, disabilities, housing and so on, as such information can be used to help local and central government plan services such as health and education.

However, not all official information is available to the public. It is quite easy to find out how many police officers are employed in your area, how many crimes were committed last year and how many were solved, because all local police authorities now have websites. But more sensitive information, such as how many officers were involved in anti-terrorist activities, is not available to the general public.

Constraints

There are a number of constraints on UK journalists: these include the **libel laws**; official secrets and anti-terrorism legislation; the **law of contempt** and other legal restrictions on court reporting; trespass, harassment and anti-discrimination legislation; laws against obscenity and blasphemy. There is also data protection and human rights legislation that relates to the right to privacy.

Most journalists operate in a competitive, commercial environment, and 'human interest' stories which generate emotive responses are guaranteed to engage readers and thus increase sales. But in reporting such stories, journalists must take care that they respect the human rights of those involved.

Political censorship

In certain parts of the world, the media are controlled by the government. This means nobody can broadcast or publish anything that contradicts government thinking or undermines the government in any way. In democratic countries, such as the UK, you are free to write and say whatever you wish, within carefully defined limits.

Under the Official Secrets Act, the UK government has the power to ban the reporting of certain subjects in all media. If a reporter wants to publish a story that may be covered by the act – usually stories about the military or the security services, the manufacture and sale of arms, the nuclear industry and so on – they must inform the government. The Official Secrets Act gives the government the power to stop the story and, in exceptional circumstances, close down the paper or TV station and arrest the reporters involved if they refuse to obey the act.

Reporting on military movement is covered by the Official Secrets Act

Discuss

"It's completely unrealistic to imagine we'll ever have *real* freedom of information in the UK. No government would ever pass a law to allow that." Do you agree or disagree?

Bloody Sunday report censored?

On Sunday 30 January 1972, British Army paratroopers shot dead 13 unarmed Catholic men during a civil rights march in Derry, Northern Ireland. Seventeen more civilians were seriously injured and one died some months later.

There was an official inquiry into what came to be known as Bloody Sunday. The soldiers claimed they were fired on before they opened fire. Civil rights marchers said the army had fired first. It was also suggested that some of the dead had been handling bombs or guns.

There have been two inquiries into the Bloody Sunday shooting. The first, the 1972 Widgery Inquiry was "deeply flawed and condemned as army propaganda" according to *The Guardian*.

A second inquiry into the shootings began in March 2000. Two journalists who used to work for *The Sunday Times* told this inquiry how their 1972 report of the Bloody Sunday shootings had been 'suppressed' by the then Lord Chief Justice. They claimed the Parachute Regiment had deliberately tried to draw the IRA into battle by attacking the civil rights march.

Reporters also criticized the newspaper for handing over their personal notebooks that included interviews and other confidential material to the Widgery inquiry without their permission.

However, another journalist, who also worked at *The Sunday Times* at the time, denied the article had been suppressed as a result of political pressure from the UK government.

There has been much disagreement over the events on Bloody Sunday, leading to suggestions that the UK government censored reports into the event

Discuss

In what sort of circumstances do you think the government might try to censor journalists and broadcasters? Do you think such censorship can be justified?

Media restrictions around the world

The oppressed press	
Iran	Several independent editors have been imprisoned and more than 30 newspapers are banned.
Liberia	Censorship, imprisonment and threats of violence are used to silence the independent media.
Zimbabwe	Journalists can be jailed for "publishing material likely to cause alarm and despondency".
Burma	It is a crime to listen to foreign radio broadcasts or use a fax machine
North Korea	Death penalty for listening to foreign broadcasts or possessing anti-government publications.
Uzbekistan	Journalists are forbidden by law to report on the discovery of new diseases.
Democratic Republic of the Congo	Death penalty for "insulting the army".

Leader Kim Jong-Il has clamped down on press freedom in North Korea by introducing media restrictions

Discuss

Discuss how dictators use censorship of the media as a way of sidelining the opposition and maintaining power.

A responsible press?

Journalistic responsibility

All journalists, whatever medium they work in, are meant to follow a code of ethics. They should aim to be honest and fair when reporting and interpreting the news, never deliberately distort the facts and, whenever possible, identify the source of their information. They should not oversimplify or report incidents out of context, and must avoid stereotyping by race, gender, age, religion and so on.

Stereotypes in magazines

There is concern about the part the media play in shaping stereotypes, such as in the way 'anorexic' female models are used in many magazines aimed at teenage girls and how they may influence readers' perceptions of a 'normal' body shape.

The content of teenage magazines is governed by a code drawn up by the Teenage Magazine Arbitration Panel (TMAP), but they have been criticized in the past. In 1996, prompted in part by explicit references to sex in *Sugar*, a group of MPs proposed a new law which would require publishers to place age suitability warnings on the covers of certain teenage magazines.

Similarly, magazines aimed at young men – so-called 'lads' mags such as *Loaded*, *FHM* and *Maxim* – have been criticized for they way they exploit images of women. A Mediawatch survey of these magazines in 2001 found that they all portray women as 'available,' like 'commodities'. One article in *Loaded* (August 2001) was illustrated with a image of a woman packaged in a pink Barbie box. Apart from articles on sex, most of these titles concentrate on 'gadgets, cars, fitness, fashion and sport'.

Chequebook journalism

It is not a criminal offence for anyone to sell their story to a newspaper or for that newspaper to buy it. However, both journalists and lawyers have expressed concern about the growing trend of **chequebook journalism**, particularly when the person selling the story is part of an on-going criminal trial. Critics argue that witnesses in an important trial may be tempted to embellish their story, in an effort to receive more money from the newspaper. If there is any evidence that the result of a trial has been affected, the judge may be forced to stop proceedings; the newspaper may then be charged with 'contempt of court' for having done something that might prejudice a fair trial.

In 1988, *The Sun* was fined for contempt of court when it claimed the defendant in an on-going rape trial was guilty. More recently, in the Damilola Taylor murder trial the judge claimed that a £50 000 reward offered by *The Daily Mail* to the key prosecution witness – a 14-year-old girl – had encouraged her to elaborate her story.

A new law has been proposed that would outlaw certain kinds of chequebook journalism. Journalists and editors who paid witnesses in criminal trials would be guilty of a criminal offence, as would witnesses who agreed to take money. Newspaper owners could also face legal bills for millions of pounds if a criminal trial were to collapse because of their involvement.

Discuss

1 In the example above, what kinds of ethical decisions were the reporters faced with? In your opinion, did they handle them well?

2 To what extent do you think lifestyle magazines form attitudes, as opposed to reinforcing existing ideas about sex and gender?

The first trial of Leeds United footballers Lee Bowyer and Jonathan Woodgate, which was stopped after a story was published by a Sunday newspaper, is thought to have cost the taxpayer £8m

Naming and shaming

In July 2000, the *News of the World* ran what came to be known as its 'naming and shaming' campaign, when it published the names and photographs of convicted sex offenders. The newspaper claimed that parents with children had a right to know who was living in their street. Following publication, there were a number of vigilante attacks. In one such attack, a man with the same name as one of the named offenders was abused in the street and had the windows of his home smashed. In another incident, a mob attacked the home of a female paediatrician – when local people assumed paediatrician and **paedophile** meant the same thing.

The campaign was widely condemned by the probation and social services, civil liberties groups and the police, who all said that the publicity drove paedophiles into hiding.

Discuss

"Naming and shaming is dangerous. It leads to trial by the media rather than trial by a court. Newspapers which name and shame are acting irresponsibly." Discuss this view.

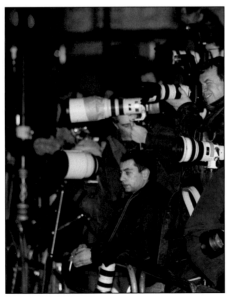

Journalists are not allowed to use long-lens cameras to obtain photographs of people in private places

The Press Complaints Commission

The **Press Complaints Commission (PCC)** is an independent body that deals with complaints from the public about the content of UK newspapers and magazines. It is the job of the PCC to enforce its Code of Practice – a set of rules agreed with the newspaper and magazine industry. The aim of the Code is to protect vulnerable groups such as children and those at risk of discrimination. In 2000 the PCC investigated 2225 complaints.

Complaints investigated by PCC in 2000

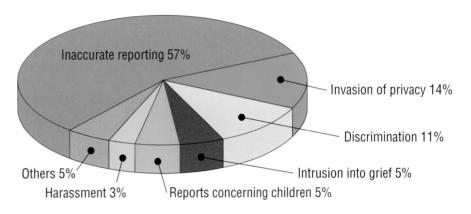

Inaccurate reporting 57%

Invasion of privacy 14%

Discrimination 11%

Intrusion into grief 5%

Reports concerning children 5%

Harassment 3%

Others 5%

PCC website – www.pcc.org.uk

Extracts from the PCC Code

- Newspapers, whilst free to be partisan, must distinguish clearly between comment, conjecture and fact.

- The use of long-lens photography to take pictures of people in private places without their consent is unacceptable. (Private places are public or private property where there is a reasonable expectation of privacy.)

- Journalists and photographers must neither obtain nor seek to obtain information or pictures through intimidation, harassment or persistent pursuit.

- Journalists must avoid publishing details of a person's race, colour, religion, sexual orientation, physical or mental illness, or disability unless these are directly related to the story.

The PCC can't award compensation. If someone feels they deserve compensation from a newspaper, they must take the paper to court. But 95 per cent of people who complain to the PCC are not wealthy celebrities. They are ordinary people, very often victims of crime, who are traumatized by the media 'spotlight,' shocked by the way their life has been turned upside down, their privacy invaded and their reputation ruined by gossip.

Reporters must strike a delicate balance between the rights of the individual to privacy, and the freedom of the press. If rich and powerful people (including politicians) feel they can 'hide' behind a privacy law, this might mean certain stories that should be told are not. This would have serious consequences for the democratic process.

In February 2002 Naomi Campbell successfully sued The Mirror for publishing a photograph of her leaving a meeting of Narcotics Anonymous. Her claim that under the new Human Rights Act, she has a right to privacy just like any other citizen was upheld by the court.

Discuss

"No one should be able to hide behind the Human Rights Act or privacy laws, especially celebrities and politicians." To what extent do you share this view?

TV, films and videos – a good or bad influence?

Couch potatoes or well-informed citizens?

As soon as the BBC began the first regular television broadcasts, in 1932, a public debate started about the social impact of the new medium – a debate that continues today. Most people nowadays would probably agree that television does influence their behaviour, but opinion is divided as to whether this influence is a positive or negative one.

Whilst the media can undoubtedly be a force for good, empowering citizens and widening their intellectual and cultural horizons, they are considered by some to be pervasive, negative influences on societies worldwide. Concerns have been expressed, for instance, about the impact of violent images in films that glamorize crime and drug-taking. Tabloid newspapers have been accused of 'dumbing down', invading people's privacy and blurring the boundary between news and entertainment.

No one would dispute the impact television has had on the way parents and children interact within the home. As more children have sets in the bedroom, viewing for them is often a solitary activity, whereas in the past it has been a social occasion and a spur to family conversation and debate. Has television created a generation of **couch potatoes**?

The first TV sets were a novelty. Proud owners would invite family and friends round to watch. Adverts for sets would include phrases such as: "Suitable for viewing by a party of up to 15"

Violence on TV and video

Do violent images on TV and in videos make viewers violent? Do viewers imitate what they see or are they progressively desensitized by lengthy exposure to screen violence? Despite thousands of studies by psychologists and social scientists to answer these questions objectively, there appears not to be an obvious link between exposure to violent images and violent behaviour.

The most comprehensive survey of research in this area was published in 1993 by America's prestigious National Academy of Sciences. It concluded that the results of this research were "uneven and ambiguous".

In 1998, the Home Office published a report entitled 'The Effects of Video Violence on Young Offenders'. This study found that offenders preferred brutal videos and identified with violent role models. But a correlation (link) between aggressive behaviour and violent entertainment does not demonstrate that one causes the other. Much depends on the background of the individual and what they bring to the act of viewing.

The Columbine High School shootings (21 April 1999), in which 13 students were shot dead by two of their schoolmates, sparked off a national debate in the US about the influence of TV and video violence. Many parents and some politicians lay the blame for the shootings at Hollywood's doorstep, especially the "testosterone-fuelled, action-filled blockbusters" of Schwarzenegger and Stallone.

However, in the ten-year period between 1990 and 2000, juvenile crime rates fell in America, whilst the same period saw a massive growth in the sale of video games, many of which have a violent content.

Some thought The Lord of the Rings – The Fellowship of the Ring *was too violent for its PG classification*

Discuss

1 "Of course violent films and TV programmes make people violent." Do you agree?

2 Do you think we need more restrictions on television violence and violent video games?

Discuss

1 Do you think there can ever be 'too much' media coverage in a free society?

2 Overall, describe whether you think the influence of the media has been positive or negative.

Soap ethics: provoking or provocative?

It isn't just reporters and editors working in the news media who are faced with important **ethical questions**. The **gatekeepers** who write, direct and produce TV soaps such as *Coronation Street* and *EastEnders* have a responsibility to consider the social impact of their programmes. This is because soaps often deal with very controversial topics such as domestic violence, rape, drug abuse and underage sex.

Coronation Street ran a storyline about a 14-year-old girl who is preyed upon by a paedophile via an internet chat room, while *EastEnders* has highlighted child abuse and domestic violence.

Programme-makers will sometimes broadcast helpline numbers at the end of an episode, so that viewers who have been upset by a particular storyline can ring and get advice and support.

Soap scriptwriters must strike a difficult balance: the storyline has to be dramatic and the characters believable, but sensitive issues must be dealt with in a responsible way. Phil Redmond, the creator of *Brookside*, believes UK soaps have become "too tabloid". They have touched on a number of strong issues, but failed to explore them in any depth. In future he wants *Brookside* to be "provoking rather than provocative".

Mental health in the media

One topic which many think the media represent irresponsibly is mental health. In 1996, the Health Education Authority analysed every article in the UK national press which mentioned mental illness. It found 46 per cent of reports linked mental illness with violent crime. Tabloid newspapers used words like "nutters", "crazies", "beasts" and "loonies" to describe mentally ill people, and featured front-page stories about "mad axemen".

The shelves of video rental stores are filled with horror films – so-called 'slasher' movies. Many of these films feature a mentally ill killer or 'psycho'. The film *Schizo*, released in 1977, had the slogan: "When the left hand doesn't know who the right hand is killing, you're dealing with a schizo".

As roughly one in six people in the UK experience mental health problems at some time in their lives, biased media representation of mental illness impacts on the lives of eight million people. Mental health charities, such as MIND, work to challenge this type of negative stereotype and claim the prejudice experienced by people with mental health problems can be more difficult to deal with than the illness itself.

> "At any one time, one adult in six suffers from one or another form of mental illness. That makes mental illness as common as asthma. But mental illness is widely misunderstood and widely feared. There is only one way to tackle public fear and misunderstanding and that is through the media.
>
> "Discrimination in any of its ugly forms – on the grounds of sex or sexual orientation, of race, or mental illness – has no place in a modern society. And it has no place in the media." Lord Wakeham, chairman of PCC, February 2000

The Broadcasting Standards Commission

The Broadcasting Standards Commission (BSC) was set up in 1996. It works as an advisory body to all broadcasters and a complaints authority for all terrestrial and satellite broadcasting media – TV and radio, text, cable and digital services. Like the ITC and PCC, it has a code of conduct and adjudicates on complaints. Like the ITC, it also carries out research into how audiences react to broadcast media. In 1998, the BSC investigated attitudes of men and women to violence on television, and found "a startling difference" between the sexes. Women felt very strongly that violence against women should be subject to stricter censorship.

The Independent Television Commission

The **Independent Television Commission (ITC)** was established in 1990. It issues licences to UK broadcasters and has a statutory responsibility to regulate programme content, as well as sponsorship and advertising on commercial television. Like the PCC (see page 19), it has a code of practice, investigates complaints and publishes its findings.

There were 4650 complaints about programme content in 2001. The ITC agreed that 1228 complaints relating to 40 programmes were valid. The ITC also received 7554 complaints about 917 different advertisements. The number of complaints about violence, sexual portrayal and language all fell during 2001. The number of complaints should be seen in the context of three million hours of broadcasting annually by all ITC licensees (see page 3).

Discuss

1 Is it the job of television soaps to 'provoke' their audience?

2 Do you think soaps deal with controversial issues in a responsible way or do they sensationalize them?

3 "It's not just people with mental health problems who are misrepresented in the media. Many other groups are too." Say why you agree or disagree with this view.

The power of advertising

Advertising

Advertising is the way organizations and individuals promote goods and services. The advertising industry is a major industry as most media depend on advertising. Without the considerable sums of money raised through advertising, many TV programmes would not get made, nor newspapers and magazines published. In 1999, UK businesses spent over £15 billion on adverts, and over 30 million adverts are published every year.

Adverts make up a large part of newspapers and magazines. These can be:
- display adverts: usually promoting big companies and using pictures and graphics to catch the reader's eye
- classified adverts: announcements placed by the general public of births, weddings, deaths and so on
- 'advertorials': adverts designed to look like the main body of the text in a newspaper or magazine. By law, they must show the words "Advertising feature" clearly.

Can brands save the world?

In Summer 2001, *The Guardian* conducted an unusual experiment. With the help of a focus group of volunteers, they created a new brand: 'Joy'. Joy was aimed at "consumers with a conscience", socially concerned citizens. Joy was sold as a product that could change the world. The unusual thing about Joy was there was no product; it was just 'an idea'.

Anti-globalization protestors often target prominent brands such as Coca-Cola, MacDonald's, Nike and Orange, accusing them of economic colonialism, of exploiting workers in developing countries, and distorting and destroying local markets.

So when thousands of *Guardian* readers responded to the Joy experiment by calling the hotline and visiting the website, this prompted Joy's creators to ask: Can brands be a force for good? Can brands save the world?

Below are examples of how two brands are trying to use their influence to bring about social change.

MTV: AIDS
- social problem: AIDS is a youth issue: of the 16 000 people that become HIV positive every day, more than half are aged 15 to 25
- diagnosis: persuade young people to change their sexual behaviour
- the brand: MTV reaches a billion people around the word and has youth credibility
- the campaign: for 20 years MTV has campaigned on AIDS, including public service announcements, artist involvement, 'Staying Alive' programming, annual sexual behaviour poll and safe sex campaigns.

Sky: Reach for the Sky
- social problem: academic studies reveal huge problems in the way Britain helps teenagers plan for their future, leading to apathy and higher education drop-out, and contributing to youth crime and alienation
- diagnosis: careers advice needs to be more inspiring, talking to teenagers in a language they relate to
- the brand: Sky is a cool brand with youth appeal, symbolizing choice and success
- the campaign: Reach for the Sky helps teenagers "see what they can be" via roadshows, workshops, a website, magazine and advertising on youth channels.

Adapted from The Guardian, *22 April 2002*

Sponsorship

Sponsorship is another important aspect of the advertising industry. News and current affairs programmes can't be sponsored, but large companies sponsor sporting events for instance, paying to have their name linked to important media events such as the FA Cup.

Many companies now sponsor programmes on commercial TV. In 2002 the American TV programme *ER*, shown on Channel 4, was sponsored by the car manufacturer, Volvo.

Television advertising is expensive – one 30-second, peak time slot can cost £25 000, so a company like Volvo will think long and hard about which programme to sponsor. They obviously thought it would enhance the image of their cars, which they market as very safe, to be linked with a programme in which doctors and nurses fight to save people's lives.

Large businesses employ advertising agencies (companies with special knowledge of the advertising industry) to create and place their adverts for them. Using extensive market research and by setting up 'focus groups', these agencies carry out research into how the public perceive products and adverts.

Advertisers are not allowed to influence the content of programmes. Commercial breaks are not permitted in religious services or schools' broadcasts. Political adverts, apart from party political broadcasts (see page 11), are also prohibited.

(see page 11)

DISCUSS

1 How might sponsors try to influence the content of programmes they are sponsoring? Why are they not allowed to do so?

2 Some people might claim that MTV's AIDS campaign is just a cynical attempt to give its brand a 'caring' image. Would you say this is a fair criticism?

Legal, honest, decent and truthful?

The **Advertising Standards Authority (ASA)** is an independent watchdog set up in 1962 to make sure that all UK non-broadcast adverts are "legal, decent, honest and truthful". The work of the ASA is paid for by a levy on display and direct mail advertising. The ASA oversees all adverts in newspapers, magazines, catalogues, direct mailing and so on. TV adverts are the responsibility of the Independent Television Commission (ITC).

When someone complains to the ASA about an advert, the ASA acts rather like a referee and decides whether or not its advertising code has been broken. All adjudications (decisions) are published on the ASA website (www.asa.org.uk). Below are details of two typical complaints.

ASA DECISION

An advert for a theatre company used a photograph of a little girl in Victorian-style dress who was pouring out a glass of champagne and had a cigarette in her mouth. Those complaining about this advert said it was "irresponsible and offensive" because it glamorized smoking and made it look attractive to children.

The ASA upheld the complaint and asked the theatre to withdraw the advert.

UPHELD

ASA DECISION

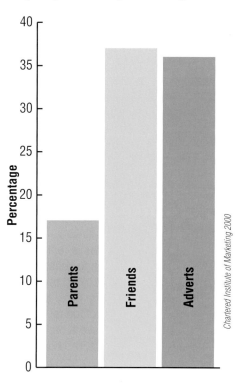

An internet security company used an image of a man holding a gun to his head, coupled with the caption: "Are you playing Russian Roulette with your company's internet access?"

Those complaining about the image said it was "offensive and distressing", particularly to anyone who had experienced the suicide of a friend or relative.

The ASA did not uphold this complaint. They argued that it was clear that the gun was a toy one and the advert was a joke, and because the leaflet was only mailed to business addresses, it was unlikely to be seen by children.

NOT UPHELD

The influence of adverts

UK adults were asked "Which has the biggest influence on children: parents, friends or adverts?" The results of the poll show that most adults believe children are greatly affected by advertising.

Chartered Institute of Marketing 2000

A group of Labour MPs wants all TV advertising to under-5s to be outlawed because they believe it amounts to 'brainwashing'. They are calling for a ban on commercial breaks during programmes for toddlers. In Sweden, TV adverts aimed at children are banned and Sweden would like to see this ban extended to other EU countries.

Discuss

"Do we really need organizations like the ASA? Isn't this just another example of 'the nanny state'? People don't need the ASA to tell them when they're being conned by an advert." Say if you agree or disagree, and why.

The growth of the internet

The internet

The **internet** is a worldwide network of computers, linked together by phone lines. Through the internet you can access the World Wide Web, communicate with others through e-mail, newsgroups and chat rooms, and create your own website. More and more people are using internet online shopping and banking services. Most access to the internet is through personal computers, with a small proportion through digital TVs or mobile phones. It is used widely in UK schools and libraries.

The internet was started in 1960 and is used by millions of people worldwide; no one is sure just how many because internet use is growing so quickly. In the UK, a survey in 2001 by the Office of National Statistics found that about 50 per cent of adults had used the internet – about 23 million adults. Young people are more likely to use it than adults. Three quarters of young people between 7 and 16 have access to the internet, and about 90 per cent say it helps them with their learning; for example, 25 per cent use online sources to aid exam revision.

Worldwide internet use

Top Ten Uses

 1 e-mail
 2 general information
 3 surfing
 4 reading
 5 hobbies
 6 product information
 7 travel information
 8 work/business
 9 entertainment and games
10 shopping

The internet is a valuable learning resource – which schools are beginning to take advantage of

The internet's potential

Because internet access is relatively inexpensive, people can communicate to a large extent without the need to satisfy advertisers or shareholders. Points of view outside the majority mainstream can be aired and debated. People can communicate and argue with others on the other side of the world, not just their immediate neighbours, creating 'communities of ideas' that are independent of geography.

The internet will have a profound effect on schooling in the future. As more and more families have PCs, the home will increasingly be the place where children access information and learn. Should schools be teaching parents how to help children to learn at home, using the internet? Schools will need to teach children how to make decisions when confronted with massive amounts of information. And children will need to learn to work with people they'll never see, people in different parts of the world, of different age groups and different cultures.

Will the internet enable us to obtain everything we want from the comfort of our own home?

The internet "will change everyday life"

THE internet is driving the biggest social and economic revolution since the 18th century, say researchers.

Thirty years on from the birth of the internet, the ferocious pace of change it has started will have as great an impact on society as factory processing and the steam engine during the industrial revolution, a new report claims.

The research, carried out by the Henley Centre for Forecasting, suggests that the internet is already having far-reaching effects on everyday life.

Electronic retailing will be the main growth area for the internet, according to the research. While most people see it primarily as a source of information, or a communication tool, more than 20 per cent believe that online shopping will be its main application within five years.

The report warns that the internet is only at the 'innovation' stage of its development. Advances in technology must move in the same direction as consumer needs. There is a feeling that people are overwhelmed by the amount of information available.

Adapted from The Guardian, *16 June 1999*

Discuss

Among your family and friends, who most uses the internet? Is there a difference in the services each of these people use? Is there one age group which has benefited more than another from the internet? Are there any drawbacks to increased internet access for some people?

Can you trust what you read on the net?

If you wanted to know about the long-term effects of smoking cannabis, you would try to consult an expert, someone who knows a lot about drugs and their effects on the body – a doctor or a forensic scientist. Or you could read an up-to-date book written by an acknowledged expert. You would probably try to talk to more than one expert and read more than one book, in case there are conflicting opinions on the subject.

Alternatively, you could search the internet for an answer. You must be very careful, however, if you do use the web. Is it clear who wrote the page? How can you tell if the information is accurate and up-to-date? Is the information presented fact or opinion? If facts are included, does the web page author tell you where they came from? If the site claims that "research shows *x* or *y*", does it say which research, who it was done by and how many subjects took part, for example?

If you do a web search and request information on "effects of cannabis", the search will offer you links to hundred of sites. Some sites provide very detailed medical and scientific information about the drug; others are dedicated to promoting the use and legalization of cannabis. Below is information taken from two sites:

Ukonline.gov.uk

The "About Us" button tells you this is an official government site, run by the Cabinet Office. It offers access to over 900 government departments. It is a searchable site and is linked to over 100 documents relating to cannabis use. The following information was accessed via one of these links, on the Scottish Drugs Forum site.

Cannabis: *Short-term Effects*

Cannabis makes you feel relaxed and, because it is a mild hallucinogen, you can find colours and sounds brighter and sharper. It can cause anxiety, affect short-term memory and make you less able to carry out complicated tasks.

Cannabis: *Long-term Effects*

If you smoke regularly or very heavily, you could have heart, lung and breathing problems, as with cigarettes. You might also feel depressed and restless. And anyone who has any mental problems should not smoke cannabis regularly.

The Scottish Drugs Forum: a non-governmental drugs information agency

Cannabis UK

The Cannabis UK website has no "About Us" button, so you have no idea who publishes it. The website presents the following information under the heading "Facts about Cannabis":

Highs Relaxation; enhanced feeling of congeniality; an aid to lateral thinking; ability to concentrate on mundane tasks; enhanced aural (hearing) awareness; midnight snacking.

Lows Continual usage can seriously weaken short-term memory and lead to lethargy, while in some people a single joint can induce paranoia, a rising pulse and dry mouth. Driving or operating heavy machinery under the influence is very stupid. Mixes badly with alcohol.

From the Cannabis UK website 2002

Who owns the internet?

Strictly speaking, nobody owns or runs the internet. A number of powerful companies such as AOL, Microsoft, Cisco and CompuServe have all played a part in putting the framework in place. There are a number of organizations concerned with the administration of the internet. These are:

- the Internet Network Information Centre (InterNIC), that registers domain names
- the Internet Society, that oversees technical standards
- the World Wide Web Consortium (W3C), that discusses the Web's programming language.

The internet began life as a secret American military computer network. Its purpose was to make the flow of military intelligence less susceptible to nuclear attack, by creating a web-like structure, which did not have one vulnerable command centre. With the end of the Cold War, the internet became more accessible, first for research organizations and universities, and then for the general public.

Cannabis has become a common recreational drug, with many users smoking joints in public places.

Discuss

1 Young people need accurate, up-to-date and impartial advice on a wide range of topics, including education, careers and health. In your opinion, is the internet a good place to obtain such information?

2 "We need to be wary of the information we get from the internet." Do you agree with this view? Give reasons.

Problems with the internet

Cyber-rights: free speech on the internet

If you wrote an article for your local newspaper full of violent racist threats, they would not publish it. If they did, they would be breaking the law. The same laws apply to publishing material on the internet, but in practice it is much harder to police internet content. It is relatively easy for anyone to open a website and publish their opinions, no matter how extreme. Once information is placed on the internet, it can be accessed by any internet user. This can lead to a number of problems.

Security

Governments are concerned that the internet could be used to spread information that is important and should be kept secret. In one case, a former MI6 agent was accused of publishing the names of many agents on the internet, causing a panic in the British security services.

Various political groups advocating violence use the web to spread their views. For example, several recent anti-globalization protests have been coordinated via the internet.

In the aftermath of the terrorist attack on New York on 11 September 2001, some people want this freedom curtailed. They believe the police should have the power to close down websites, and intercept and read e-mails.

Other security problems could come from the spread of computer viruses via e-mail. Governments worry that terrorists could send computer viruses to attack government services, such as water and electricity supplies.

The internet allows activists to coordinate their protest activity

Pornography

Many people are also concerned about pornography on the net. A survey revealed that 60 per cent of UK schools take steps to prevent students from accessing pornographic material, but only 25 per cent of parents use net 'filters'. One in ten young children claims to have found material they described as upsetting whilst browsing. There have been instances, too, of sex offenders using chat rooms to make contact with children.

Advocates of internet freedom, whilst sharing the concerns that many parents have about violent and pornographic material, are opposed to any kind of web censorship. They claim it is easy to get involved in an emotive debate about children and pornography, and lose sight of the benefits of the web. They argue that the internet is helping to erode the power of global media monopolies by promoting the idea that "everyone is a reader, everyone is a writer".

Hacking

Another problem is hacking. A hacker is someone who tries to enter the computer system of another person, company or government, without their permission. Areas that are locked with passwords are regarded as a challenge by hackers, who can usually solve the passwords.

In one recent case, a Russian computer hacker entered the computer system of America's largest bank, Citicorp. He managed to steal more than £8 million through the computer system before he was caught.

Computer hacking on the increase

COMPANIES frequently downplay the threat they face from attacks conducted via the internet, but the spectre of online crime seems real enough.

Computer hacking, the term widely used for illegally breaking into a computer system, is growing, with internet attacks up by 64 per cent in the first half of 2002.

Between January and June 2002 more than one million attempts were made to hack into websites or take them offline, of which 180 000 succeeded, according to internet security company Riptech.

US telecoms company AT&T warned employees last week to look out for attempts to steal company secrets, as a major hacking conference called H2K2 was being held in New York. The annual event frequently includes an attack on a high-profile computer system.

The concerns look justified. On Thursday night the online version of American national newspaper *USA Today* was hacked resulting in seven spoof news pages – including its front page – being added to its website. The false stories included an Iraqi missile attack on Israel and the Vatican proclaiming that the Bible was a hoax.

More sinister hacking attempts are also becoming more frequent. Carratu International, a private investigation company, said it had experienced a 50 per cent increase in hacking-related work this year.

Within the last month it has been hired by a UK venture capital company, an overseas bank and a law firm, all of which have had their computer systems breached.

Adapted from The Daily Telegraph, *16 July 2002*

Big Brother law

11 February 2000 – The UK government has just announced its plans to allow law enforcement agencies to access e-mail correspondence.

For the first time, UK police will legally be able to read private e-mails and listen in on wireless phone conversations.

While using the new bill as a way to crack down on the distribution of offensive and illegal material on the internet is supported by most citizens, some are still worried that these new powers could be used against people.

According to the bill, failure to hand over a text-only copy of a suspicious e-mail or refusing to give police access to the encryption key you are using could result in a two-year prison sentence.

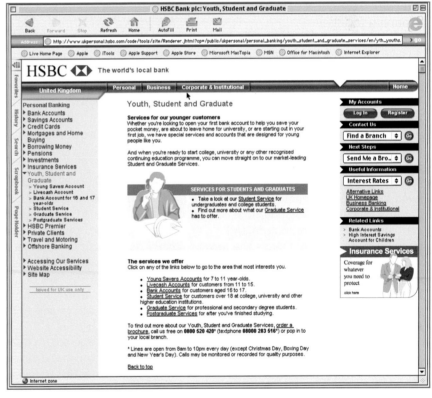

Discuss

1 Some people see the internet as potentially very dangerous because it affords people the opportunity to air the most extreme views. Do you think this freedom should be curtailed?

2 Internet banking and online shopping are growing very fast. Do you think that hacking might jeopardize these and other internet-based commerce?

The digital revolution

The digital future

The present analogue method of transmitting TV and radio signals is gradually being replaced by a digital system. This change will expand broadcasting capacity enormously. Digital broadcasting uses computer technology to create signals that have to be decoded before a TV set can turn them into sound or pictures. To receive digital TV, therefore, you need a set-top box or television that will decode these signals. Likewise, you will require a digital radio set to receive digital radio.

The legal framework governing the transition from analogue to **digital broadcasting** is in the Broadcasting Act 1996. This act allows for the provision of a number of new digital TV and radio channels, and determines how they will be licensed. The government has yet to announce a 'switch-off date' for existing analogue channels, but hopes the transition will be complete by 2010.

Digital TV and radio

Digital TV signals are received through an existing aerial, cable or satellite dish. Digital TV will provide improved reception, more channels and extra features, such as interactive channels with home shopping facilities.

A digital radio will allow you to receive sound (for example, pop music) and data (via a liquid crystal display, LCD) simultaneously. The LCD might tell you what track is being played, the title of the CD, provide additional information about the artist, and up-to-date news of similar artists and CDs. An on-screen menu will allow you to select the kind of information you want from a range of options.

It is this interactive potential, coupled with superior picture and sound quality, that will make the new digital media so powerful.

Digital TV and radio will also have an impact on the way you receive local, national and international news. In the 'digital' future, a newsroom will act more like an information publisher. In the morning, it will present the news on television, as well as on radio (for viewers who have left home and are driving to work). During the day, the news will be on the internet for people at work with access to PCs. In the evening, the news will be published on cable, over the air and via satellite. The newsroom will continuously update local news and information available on demand.

Broadband technology

Another development which is having a major impact on the future of the media is **broadband technology**. This technology allows media companies to transmit huge amounts of information at very high speeds into, and between, businesses and homes. Broadband connections makes internet access around 40 times faster. A broadband connection means that your PC can be permanently online, allowing you to be constantly connected to the internet. Because of this, you can be alerted instantly as soon as you receive an e-mail.

Media analysts also believe that in future the family television will function more like a computer – enabling you, via the internet, to shop, carry out all your banking and financial transactions, and download videos and games. This convergence of interactive technologies will also mean you will be able to send video e-mails to family and friends.

At present you are used to thinking of a TV, a computer and a mobile phone as separate items, but convergence will change all that. A phone could be a miniature TV, a camera and a computer. This means that in a few years time everyone could have their own pocket internet terminal. The technology that has made this possible is WAP (wireless application protocol), which gives mobile handsets much more capacity to handle data than they have now.

Mobile phone technology is constantly developing, and mobile phone use is becoming more widespread

Intelligent systems

The growth in digital technology means that not only are household appliances getting faster, they are also getting smarter, and smaller. For example, a new wave of digital video recorders was launched in the UK in 2002. Unlike a traditional video recorder, these 'TV organizers' have no tapes. Instead, they use a hard disc, which can record up to 20 hours of television programmes.

Because TV organizers are intelligent, they build a database from your viewing habits. Digital technology then allows the TV organizers to communicate with the computers of cable and satellite companies which provide your TV programmes. The result is that the TV organizer will analyse future TV programmes and record the ones it thinks you will like. Output sockets allow programmes then to be recorded by a traditional video recorder, or even to be played and stored digitally on your computer.

Meanwhile, the first 'TV glasses' were launched to the general public in the UK in 2002. These consist of two small screens built into the glasses, connected to a set of small headphones. What could this mean for the future? Perhaps, a family sitting together in their living room, but all watching different TV programmes using different sets of glasses.

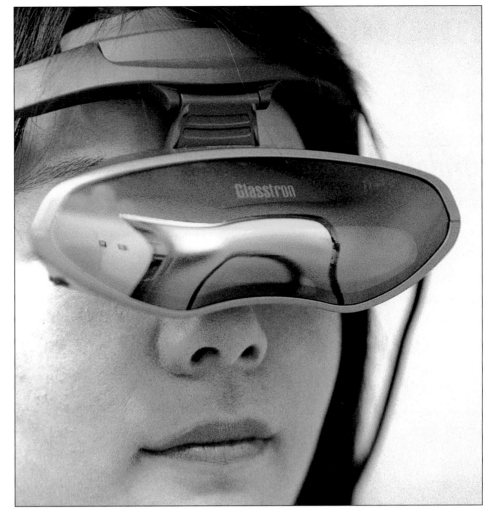

One of the many styles of 'TV glasses' available in 2002

Discuss

Digital technologies mean media companies can target smaller audiences. This has clear benefits for advertisers, but does it have any benefits for viewers and listeners?

More choice

One consequence of convergence is **audience segmentation**. In the early days of radio and TV, listeners and viewers had a very restricted choice of programmes. Programme makers needed to devise programmes that would appeal to a very wide audience – all ages, all ethnic and social groups. The digital, interactive age will make possible 'tailor-made' schedules, that will allow you to decide what you want to see and hear, and when. This new technology means advertisers can target groups of consumers very precisely, and make their campaigns more cost effective. It also means that TV producers can create more specialized TV channels that appeal to a particular audience. The recent growth of cable TV channels such as the Sci-Fi Channel, the History Channel and the Shopping Channel is evidence of this.

As audiences fragment, and programme providers cater for a wider range of diverse viewing groups, ratings figures for certain programmes are bound to fall. For example, only 6.3 million viewers watched the 2002 FA Cup Final, compared to 32 million in 1970. As more people get their news online, it is predicted that ratings for traditional BBC/ITV evening news bulletins will decline.

Informing the world – who sets the global agenda?

Bridging the digital divide

Some global media analysts argue that the world economy is fast becoming an information economy. Information is now a 'commodity', to be bought and sold. Analysts claim that this new information economy is dividing citizens into those who are 'information-rich' and those who are 'information-poor', meaning they cannot afford the information they need to improve their lives.

Annan wants "information for all"

The United Nations secretary general Kofi Annan has urged leaders of the international television industry to play their role in bridging the digital divide between rich and poor countries.

Mr Annan told them that whilst there are 1.5 billion television sets and 2.5 billion radios in the world, only five per cent of people have access to the internet.

Amongst those attending the meeting was the director-general of the BBC, Greg Dyke. Mr Dyke said the world wasn't globalizing, it was Americanizing. He said services such as BBC World Service radio, BBC World TV and the BBC's Online News were vitally important in order to prevent the largest player, the US, dominating and dictating the international news agenda.

Fernando Espuelas from Star Media Network, a leading internet brand in Latin America, compared the arrival of the internet to the French Revolution as a critical moment in human history. He believes it should be made available to everyone.

Discuss

1 Do you think the world is being 'Americanized' rather than globalized?

2 *New Internationalist* claims corporate media are "biased". Why do you think it says this? What does the article tell you about Indymedia that suggests it may be able to counter this bias? Does the article imply Indymedia is unbiased?

Indymedia

Indymedia – the Independent Media Centre (IMC) – made its remarkable debut during the Seattle protests against the World Trade Organization in November 1999. Since then over two million people have accessed its website to get a grassroots view of events receiving biased and unreliable coverage in the corporate media.

The initiative was born out of frustration with the way mainstream media sensationalize or ignore the almost daily anti-globalization protests occurring around the world. Media activists created a forum for continual up-to-the-minute reports as well as local perspectives on the issues.

Over the past year IMC has grown exponentially. It now has an international network of over 44 'people's newsrooms'.

Power is decentralized. Indymedia uses free software that allows anyone to self-publish content instantly onto its internet newswires. While connected to a vast alternative media network, each centre is autonomous.

The New York City IMC, for example, has highly active newswire on its website, a monthly newspaper and a video team that compiles footage into several documentaries. Now it's about to launch the first permanent Indymedia web radio station.

In Israel, media activists are providing critical perspectives on the army's abuses of Palestinians in the Middle East crisis, while in Chiapas, Mexico, a new Indymedia centre has been set up to report on the indigenous Zapatista struggle.

A myriad of visions and missions make up the Indymedia mix, which is largely defined by who decides to participate, how much time they have and what they want to make of it. Those working on the international network are still working out how to put the pieces of the Indymedia puzzle together. A major issue is that in the North access to the web is easier than in the South.

Adapted from New Internationalist, April 2001

Colonization by TV

Does the explosion of Western satellite television stations undermine values and cultures in the developing world, or is it a welcome step in the information age? Should Western media be controlled?

According to the views expressed on the BBC online bulletin board, 46 per cent of people agree that Western media should be controlled, whilst 54 per cent believe it should not be controlled.

The bulletin board below represents a selection of those opinions expressed.

Discuss

Do you think Western media are undermining the values and cultures in the developing world?

Communal TVs are beginning to appear in villages in less economically developed countries such as in Africa

Is television a colonizing force? Absolutely. Should it be controlled? Absolutely not. The most we can hope for is that the flow of information will be two-way…that both cultures will learn something from one another.

Ash Black, US

It's both a threat to national culture and, for different reasons, a threat to totalitarianism. Better let people watch what they want. And I don't believe it's pornography that the Saudi regime is worried about (that's just an excuse). What they're really worried about is unfiltered news.

Elwood, Brazil

Yes, most definitely Western media should be regulated or even eliminated in the countries of the Developing World. The Western media have in no way contributed to the promotion or survival of Godly values. It has led to the deterioration of society in general. The 'soaps' are the main tool of incitement and adds sheer garbage to anyone's intellect. The world news is also biased. Each country should analyse world events through their own eyes, not through the dominant Western eyes.

Harsini Wickramasuriya, Bridgetown, Barbados

No, a free press is necessary for a democracy to work. When governments start controlling the media, the people of that country have no way of knowing what is the truth and what isn't. Freedom does not mean that no one will be offended or hurt, it means that people will be able to control their own lives and (as long as they don't hurt other people) do what they want to do.

Richard T. Ketchum, US

I feel very strongly that Western media should be controlled, with some exceptions in relation to news and current affairs. It is too easy, and it appears cheaper, for broadcasters to buy programmes, rather than developing them for themselves. Thus different cultures don't develop their own ideas and identities, and I feel become clones of the culture they watch on the box. Scary (and particularly noticeable with the kids). I value the diversity of the world, and I can see it getting eroded very quickly due to the effect of Western media. Is there a workable solution?

Stephen Hurton, Australia

BBC News website, 14 January 1999

Index and glossary

Advertising Standards Authority (ASA)
An independent body that monitors all UK non-broadcast adverts (see page 23).

Analogue channels
Existing channels, such as BBC 1 and ITV, which use technology soon to be replaced by digital transmission (see page 2).

Audience segmentation
The splitting of an audience into smaller units, using specifically targeted media (see page 29).

Biased reporting
Reporting influenced by factors such as personal preference, prejudice, censorship (see page 14).

Broadband technology
A method of transmitting large amounts of digital information at very high speeds (see pages 2, 28).

Broadcasting Standards Commission (BSC)
The group set up by Parliament to look into complaints about TV and radio (see page 21).

Broadsheet
A newspaper printed on large sheets of paper – e.g. The Times (see pages 4, 8)

Censorship
Control of what the media prints or broadcasts by government of other powerful groups (see page 16).

Chequebook journalism
The practice of journalists paying large amounts of money to individuals to obtain 'exclusive' stories (see page 18).

Couch potatoes
A person who does very little besides watching television – a TV 'addict' (see page 20).

Cross-media ownership
The ownership by a single company of different types of media (see page 7).

Digital broadcasting
A way of transmitting better pictures and sound more quickly (see page 28).

Digitally manipulated photographs
Images that have been altered after they have been taken, using a computer (see page 15).

Ethics/ethical questions
A code of behaviour describing our rights and responsibilities (see page 21)

Fast news
News stories given a lot of media coverage as soon as they break (see page 13).

Gatekeepers
Editors and others who select the information that appears in a range of media (see pages 8, 21).

Human interest story
A news story, usually about 'ordinary' people, rather than celebrities or politicians (see page 12).

Hype
Exaggeration, overstatement, stretching the truth (see page 13).

Independent Television Commission (ITC)
The body that grants TV licences to UK broadcasters, and regulates their programmes (page 21).

Indymedia
An independent web-based group that monitors media bias (see page 30).

Information poor
People and countries that can't afford to access information via the new technologies such as the internet (see page 30).

Internet
A global system of communication between personal computers (see page 24).

Law of contempt
The law which forbids journalists and others making comments that could influence an ongoing court case, such as a murder trial (see page 16).

Libel laws
The laws that stop the publication of lies about an individual (see page 16).

Media feeding frenzy
A large number of journalist reporting the same story at length (see page 13).

Negative campaigning
Political opinions, including adverts, that focus exclusively on an opponent's faults (see page11).

New media
All information obtained via the internet (see page 1).

Paedophile
An adult who commits sexual offences against children (see page 19).

Party Political Broadcasts
Broadcasts used by political parties to explain their policies (see page 11).

Press Complaints Commission (PCC)
The organization which deals with complaints about all UK newspapers and magazines (see page 19).

Public relations firms
Companies employed to promote the success or 'image' of an individual or organisation (see page 10).

Public watchdog
An organisation, set up by the government, to supervise another organisation, to ensure it does its job fairly and effectively (see page 3).

Regional media
Local newspapers, TV and radio stations (see page 5).

Slow news
News stories that get minimal media coverage over a long period (see page 13).

Spin doctor
A person paid to manipulate the media – often employed by political parties (see page 10).

Sponsorship
Advertising in which companies pay to have their name shown at major events or in association with special broadcasts (see page 22).

Tabloid
A newspaper with pages half the size of a broadsheet (see pages 4, 8).

Terrestrial television
Stations that send and receive signals without the use of satellites (see page 2).